THE PARALLAX

The Parallax

See Yourself with New Understanding

Donald R. Rickert, PhD

abbott press®
A DIVISION OF WRITER'S DIGEST

The Parallax
See Yourself with New Understanding

ISBN: 978-1-4582-0058-7 (sc)
ISBN: 978-1-4582-0057-0 (e)
ISBN: 978-1-4582-0059-4 (hc)
Library of Congress Control Number: 2011916502

Abbott Press books may be ordered through booksellers or by contacting:

Abbott Press
1663 Liberty Drive
Bloomington, IN 47403
www.abbottpress.com
Phone: 1-866-697-5310

Printed in the United States of America

Abbott Press rev. date: 9/21/2011

For Sharen

Death leaves heartache, no one can heal;

Love leaves a memory no one can steal.

Irish Proverb

1

Through the Years ...

you toss and turn at night. It's no longer dreams that keep you awake; it's memories. As you go about your day, these memories consume you; regret, guilt, pain, and grief drift over you like disconnected shadows. But they're yesterdays' realities, and their manifestations are ghosts. They no longer exist; however, they persist, attempting to take form. You tell yourself that *they can't hurt you*, but you fear they already have, finding ways to lurk in the present until you exorcise them, releasing their power over you, giving you peace.

You question how you got to this place, hoping that a trickster might be blamed, suspecting that you've been led unwittingly to this point. But you fear that's not the case, knowing that oblivion of time, cloaked by obsession and naiveté, has guided your journey, and now malevolent spirits threaten you, nurtured by remorse left like crumbs along a darkened path.

You remember the exhilaration that you felt as you began your journey, looking toward the horizon, yearning fulfillment, but your path took unexpected twists and turns, revealing apparitions that threaten your hope.

You know you are flawed. And, although you have always known this fact, you hoped somehow you'd escape the consequences of your imperfection. Without malice, you made mistakes that you can't correct, some by neglect, some with forethought. Being sorry is insufficient. So you try to forget.

You have few choices. You're mortal, trapped in a physical body, and you, along with those you love, get hurt. Emotions can be unforgiving demons, impossible to ignore. Your survival demands that you free yourself from your fears and save your soul.

You're encouraged to confront your ghosts and are told that you'll find answers through writing. *Words have power.* You're told that if you gather your courage and transfer your fears onto the page, you can escape their grip. You're promised peace. As you listen, the words you hear reverberate in your mind. *The cost of inertia is too great to ignore.* Stories begin to reveal themselves like nesting Matuska dolls, melding with your consciousness as if your own.

Clasping hands, they walked. Oblivious

to the world. Cherishing
each other. Yearning
connection. Revealing
shared hope. Trusting

two points converge on the horizon.

2

The Parallax

I piled some kindling into the moss-rock fireplace and warmed my hands as the dry pine burst into flames, breaking the chill of the September mountain air. I looked around the oak-timbered room. Massive floor-to-ceiling windows framed snow-capped peaks that towered above the valley.

It was dark when we'd arrived, so we hadn't fully appreciated the view. It was everything I'd hoped for. Soon Sarah would wake up and walk into the room. I could hardly wait to see her expression when she looked out the massive windows.

I knew she'd be pleased because coming to the mountains had been her idea. She wanted to celebrate our twenty-fifth wedding anniversary in Rocky Mountain National Park, so I rented a cabin on the southern slope of Prospect Mountain on the outskirts of Estes Park, Colorado, and spared no expense in planning our return. Katie, our daughter, would be with us, flying in from Atlanta just before noon. We'd planned a leisurely ride back to the cabin, knowing she'd enjoy the aspens' display of color along the vast meadows near Nederland.

I took a deep breath as I looked out the window. The fall color had come early. Across the valley, patches of gold, surrounded by lush green pine, covered the mountain slopes: The Crags, Twin Sisters, Lily Mountain, Estes Cone, Mt Lady Washington, and Giantrack. I knew them all. But what I didn't see impacted me most. Longs Peak was hidden behind a wall of clouds. I clicked on the remote for the cabin's large flat screen television to check the weather report.

When I first saw the breaking news, I half-thought that the broadcast was an Orson Welles kind of thing—a contemporary *War of the Worlds* marketing stunt. Transfixed by the news, I turned up the volume, as if loudness would add clarity.

Sarah came into the room and said something, but I couldn't hear what she said above the blaring sound. She clasped my hand, but without thinking, I pulled away and moved closer to the screen, still trying to gather my senses.

Images of the Twin Towers, burning and collapsing, played and replayed on the breaking news coverage. I stood motionless for several minutes before I noticed that Sarah was sitting on the couch sobbing.

I muted the sound. "I'm sorry, what?"

"Katie's plane's in the air."

Still dazed, I said, "Whatever's happened, it seems to be limited to New York, nowhere else." A news alert crawled across the bottom of the screen. Another plane had crashed into the Pentagon and another into a field in Pennsylvania.

I grabbed the bottle of whiskey that we'd brought along for our celebration, my favorite single-malt—Talisker. Its peaty flavor is best appreciated when sipped, but with the world collapsing around me, nuance had lost its allure. I slugged a drink from the bottle, as I slumped onto the large overstuffed chair. When we'd arrived, I'd claimed the chair as mine and moved it next to the windows, so I'd have view of both the mountains and the television. I looked out the window. Longs Peak was still shrouded from view.

Scaling that mountain had once seemed like an important challenge. I'd even hoped that Sarah and I might hike to its summit together someday. It's a difficult trail, rising 5,200 feet above the trailhead. I figured it would take two days, but it would be worth it. We'd hike to the tree line the first day and then get up before dawn, planning to reach the peak the second day before the afternoon storms, knowing that lightning strikes are a danger above the tree line. Better yet, the guidebook promised that if you start out on the trail beyond the canopy of pine trees before sunrise, flashlights from other hikers ahead on the trail *flicker like fireflies.* I'd always wanted to be with Sarah to see those flickering lights. I gulped another drink from the bottle and sank back into my chair.

Sarah shot a disapproving glance at me and set an empty glass on the end table next to me. "Frank, if you must drink, use a glass."

I filled the glass to the rim. She hadn't taken any of this well. She needed agreement, harmony and happy endings— literally. If she didn't like the ending of a movie, she'd rewrite it on the way home from the theater. *It should've ended like ... or I think ... happens next* or *I bet later they'll* ... In her world,

11

Rick would marry Ilsa after the war—*some people are just meant for one another.* She forced a smile and walked away. I took another gulp of whiskey.

Sarah pointed to the fireplace. "Can't you smell that?"

I'd started a fire when I got up but neglected it after I saw the news. Half-charred kindling smoldered beneath the grate. I knelt down and blew across the embers until the log reignited. Even that slight exertion, at Estes Park's lofty elevation, left me feeling dizzy and a bit queasy. I sat down and took another drink, swirling it in my mouth to get rid of the sour, acid taste that lingered from the late-night pizza delivery we'd eaten when we arrived the evening before.

Sarah grabbed her cell phone. "CNN said the airlines grounded flights that haven't departed. They say there could be terrorists on some of the planes still in the sky. Please call Delta."

"I tried ... couldn't get through." I stared out the window. Outside, people walked along the hiking trail that wove through the grove of aspen trees in front of the cabin as if nothing had happened. Didn't they care? *Keep your priorities straight.* That's what my father would have told me. I couldn't imagine what he'd be thinking now.

Sarah tossed the phone onto the sofa. "Isn't she supposed to land soon? Do you..."

"Damn." I pounded my fist on the end table, accidentally slopping whiskey out of my glass. I'm a cop. I needed to be in control, but there was absolutely nothing that I could do. I looked at Sarah and then at the muted television.

Sarah grabbed a napkin and blotted up the spilled whiskey. "Frank, I know you're upset, but the news said to stay calm. You'll feel better when Katie gets here. We'll be together."

But we wouldn't be *together.* We had two children—Katie and Ryan, and one of them wouldn't be here. Ryan had decided to stay in Atlanta. Sarah paced back and forth across the room, fidgeting with the necklace that I'd given her on our wedding day. I asked, muting my words so much that they might have well been thoughts, "Why couldn't Ryan have come?" She didn't answer.

It was an unnecessary question. Sarah always defended our children's decisions. In retrospect, she behaved much like my mother did when I was a child. I suppose my father had similar frustrations with me even though I always tried to live up to his expectations.

Once when I was at scout camp, Dad sent me a handwritten letter. After I got home, I tucked it away with my stamp collection. Mom sent a letter too, but I didn't save hers. I guess I expected things like that from Mom.

Dad's handwriting was as unexpected as the letter itself —long, curving ink strokes that brushed across the page. I think it was the first time I'd seen anything that he'd written. It surprised me. His pen strokes captured a part of him that his sternness had hidden, a sternness that manifested itself with his never failing to tell me how to live my life. He called his rules *taking the high road.*

Sarah finally stopped pacing, as if she'd just realized that I'd asked a question, and grabbed a CD from a rack in the bookcase. "Hey, look what I found—Elvis. Come sit with me. We'll listen to some music." She slid the CD into the stereo and said, "Does it seem like twenty-five years?"

If Sarah was anxious about something, she'd change the subject. She did it all the time. She'd usually talk about sentimental things, special moments, like how we first met, the Elvis concert in St. Louis—her favorite story.

Our meeting was pure chance, but Sarah would call it fate. I'd won two tickets to see Elvis at Kiel Auditorium in St. Louis from a contest that the KXOK radio station had sponsored. The odds were stacked against our meeting because if I'd known that the prize was a pair of tickets to see Elvis, I wouldn't have called. I wasn't an Elvis groupie, but I decided to go solo and sell the second ticket at the gate. I'd have some laughs and make a couple of bucks. As it turned out, I nailed it. I sold my ticket for three times the face value to some kook who fit right in with everyone who flocked to see the *King*. Unfortunately, I forgot that I'd end up having to sit next to him all night. It was a bizarre crowd—grandmas and stoners.

Elvis closed the show by crooning one of his typical love songs and sent a flurry of gold scarves into the crowd. One of those scarves fluttered onto the back of the seat in front of me. As I reached for it, the girl who had been sitting there turned to grab for it. Her long brown hair swept a floral scent across my face, and when I looked into her dark-brown eyes, I felt them consume me.

I stammered, trying to say something clever. As I hesitated, a large gray-haired woman grabbed the scarf. When the old women turned away, the girl raised her shoulders, puffed out her cheeks and swayed side to side as if waddling, pantomiming the large women's movements as she burst into gasps of laughter. She told me that her name was Sarah and that she also won her tickets from KXOX.

After the concert, we ended up side-by-side, moving together with the crush of people that pushed toward the exits. It was then that we discovered that we'd both be at Southern Illinois University in the fall. I'd be starting my third year as a criminal justice major and she'd be a freshman. After that night, I wished that I could have spent every minute with her. A month later, I asked her to marry me.

Her reaction was more than I'd expected. She was only eighteen and I was twenty-two, so I figured we'd have a long engagement and get married after we finished college. But she told me that she wanted to get married immediately, vying for a June wedding. However, it was 1976, and I was sure that if we got married anywhere near the Fourth of July we couldn't escape the embarrassment of being labeled a *Yankee Doodle* couple for the rest of our lives. I convinced her that we should wait at least until the fall, thinking the bicentennial celebrations would have subsided by then.

I could tell my suggestion disappointed her, but it only took a minute before her spirits surged again. She told me that September would be a great time to get married. In September, there'd be less chance of rain, the evenings would be cooler, and there'd be less hassle getting a hall for a reception. We settled on Saturday, September 11th.

I grabbed the cell-phone and tried to call again. A dissonant buzz grated in my ear. "No use, still busy." Visibly shaken, Sarah's arms dropped to her side, and the CD case slipped to the floor.

I raised the glass of whiskey, emptying the last swallow, and got up from my chair, wanting to be closer to her. But instead, I stumbled, nearly falling before steadying myself on the arm of the sofa and lowering myself back down, regretting slugging the whiskey.

"Frank, are you okay? Listen, it's our song *Can't Help Falling in Love with You*. Remember?" She sang along with the music.

I said, "I can't believe that you're singing—not now."

She stopped singing. "You should talk."

"Whatever..."

"Dammit, Frank. We can't help what's happening. Today's our anniversary. We're here now. We should try to stay calm like they said."

"I can't."

"We could try."

I didn't want to argue with her but found it difficult to join in on her denial. I noticed she was wearing her hiking boots. I said, "What's with the boots?"

She looked down, as if confused. "Oh, I forgot. When I woke up, before I saw what was happening, I thought we'd go for a hike." She sat down and unlaced her boots and said, "Guess not," as she pulled one off, tossed it at my feet, and smiled. "Besides, they're not just hiking boots, they're your *gotta haves*— your precious Kraines. You surely haven't forgotten about our Kraines."

I stoked the fire, reigniting the flame. She was right, I remembered. We bought our Kraines soon after we were married. I not only remembered what I'd said, but I remembered how I'd said it— with the same sarcasm that seemed to shadow me throughout my life.

We lived off campus which helped us stay focused and avoid the distractions that plagued our friends—parties, drugs, and booze.

I'd been reading an article, *Kraine Sales Take Flight*, in the newspaper while we were eating breakfast and getting ready for class. In a show of faux enthusiasm, I slammed my fist on the kitchen table and shouted. "Gotta have them."

Sarah nearly choked on her orange juice. I'd startled her. "Gotta have what?"

"Kraines... This article says that Colorado shoemaker Wilmer Kraine makes handcrafted hiking boots that are made so well he can't keep up with all his orders. But he refuses to increase his prices."

She said, "You want hiking boots?"

"Why not, we could both get a pair."

I had always wanted to go to the mountains, and because Sarah had wanted to have our wedding reception at Giant

City State Park near the SIU campus, I expected she'd feel the same. My dad had told me stories he'd heard from his father, who had immigrated to America in 1938 when my father was a boy. Dad always talked about my grandfather's home in Königsee, Germany. He said that when he was a boy, they'd hike along the mountain trails to a scenic spot where they'd have lunch while my grandfather told him stories of the Bavarian Alps. He said we'd go to the mountains someday but we never did.

Images of the collapsing towers continued on the television in an unrelenting loop. I couldn't believe we were talking about hiking boots when so many people had died. "Yes, those are our Kraines. Why?"

"I just remember that you had to have the perfect pair of boots."

"They were good boots." I looked at Sarah. She hadn't changed. Her eyes always revealed her emotions. "Don't you remember our first trip to the Rockies—our hike to Emerald Lake?"

"Just that you had more fun planning than hiking."

She was right. I'd bought a hiking guide and planned everything. I still had the guide and had brought it along for our return. I grabbed it and looked at its tattered cover. A handful of pictures were tucked in the back of the book. One of the pictures was from that trip—Sarah standing on a boulder on the shore of a mountain lake with her hands on her hips, beaming with pride. I'd picked the hike to Emerald Lake because I'd read in my hiking guide that the Nymph Lake/Emerald Lake Trail was nearly perfect.

As we started up the trail that day, I told Sarah that in the 1920's young girls were hired by the Park Service to dress in fairy costumes and sit along the shore of Nymph Lake— art deco, *au naturel*. But after I told her the story, I wished I hadn't. When we were out of sight of the other hikers, she launched into a ballerina pose, curled her index finger and beckoned me with a seductive Bette Davis-look in her eyes. *I'm all yours.* I grimaced, thinking other hikers were on the trail and I didn't want anyone to see us acting so foolishly.

When Sarah saw my reaction to her playfulness, she slumped from her pose and her smile evaporated. She took out a cigarette, frowning as she stuffed the empty package into her jeans pocket. "You don't have one spontaneous bone in your body."

As I marched ahead, I said, "I'm sorry. I just thought we should get going. Come on. This trail's a piece of cake."

"Oh yeah, then see if you can catch me." She ran past me.

"And if I catch you—"

"I guess we'll have to play that by ear." She ran ahead but stopped when she reached a section of trail covered with snow.

My trail guide had indicated that the trail to Emerald Lake was only moderately difficult in the summer, but I'd forgotten that summer comes late at higher altitudes. Regardless, I wasn't going to let anything deter my plan. I stomped my foot into the snow leaving a waffle shaped impression. "Now this is more like it."

Sarah trudged on. "The air is so cold up here. It takes my breath away."

I reached the lake after tromping through the ankle-deep snow for thirty minutes. Sarah arrived several minutes later and climbed up onto a boulder and stood on top, looking like an Olympic champion reveling in her success. That's when I snapped the picture.

I handed the picture to Sarah and tossed another log onto the fire. The logs popped and cracked as the fire blazed. "You were always the comedian. I still remember what you said when you climbed up onto that boulder:

Emerald Lake— what a gem. I'm just lucky that *Saturday Night Live* didn't snatch you up before I did. But then, I didn't marry you for your jokes."

Sarah's smile faded and her body stiffened. "I really felt that I'd accomplished something. And besides, it was the only hike that you took with our Kraines. When we hiked to Odessa Lake, you had to have new boots.

It had been years since we'd spoken of the hike to Odessa. It was an awful hike that I just wanted to forget.

Sarah grabbed the hiking guide and took the other pictures from the flap, thumbing through them frantically, seeming to know exactly what she was looking for. "Here it is. Look at Mr. Perfect—with his *perfect* boots—his *new* boots."

The picture was of me, sitting on the bank of a lake with my boots off, rubbing my feet, grimacing. I put the picture back behind the flap and shoved the book back at her. As she reached for it, a dried aspen leaf fell from between the pages and fluttered to the floor. I reached for the book, but the effects of the whiskey had caught up with me, stumbling, I stepped on the leaf, crushing it.

Sarah knelt on the floor, attempting to gather up the crushed pieces. "You've ruined it. After all these years—it's gone." She began to cry.

I looked away. "It's just a dried up leaf."

Sarah stood and stepped toward me, her face flushed red as she said, "You're right. It didn't mean anything. Saving it didn't mean anything. Our trip to Odessa Lake didn't mean anything. So how can I expect that being here now means anything?" She turned away.

My body felt limp. I braced myself against the back of the chair, wishing that I'd listened to her and had stopped drinking sooner. But it wasn't the whiskey that made me forget the leaf. I'd simply forgotten. Why had she wanted a keepsake from that awful trip?

After the hike to Emerald Lake, we hadn't hiked again until we returned to the Park fourteen years later. Sarah had often told me that she wanted to return to the Rockies. But each time she'd ask, I'd find an excuse to say no.

However, that particular time she insisted on returning to Rocky Mountain National Park, saying that after fifteen years we needed some time alone, suggesting a trip to the Park would be like a second honeymoon— *just the two of us.*

After I finished my degree and graduated from police academy, we moved to Atlanta where I'd been offered a job on the Atlanta P.D. The move had been difficult for Sarah. Until we were married she'd never been away from her family, so the ten-hour drive to southern Illinois made Atlanta seem a lifetime away. I knew that the stress of my job often resulted in my being detached, and to make things worse, she was pregnant with Ryan when we'd moved and had to put off finishing her degree. Three years later Katie was born. Looking back, I realize how isolated she must have felt, but unfortunately, I didn't think about it until she pushed so hard for us to take that trip. And even after my belated realization, I made some bad choices.

Sarah's parents had agreed to babysit, so we dropped the kids off with them and drove to Colorado for our second trip to the mountains, planning to camp at Glacier Basin in Rocky Mountain National Park. The first hike we took was to Odessa Lake.

As we'd started up the trail that day, I thought of what Sarah had said when she pleaded with me to return to the mountains—*just the two of us,* but all I could think of was the work that would be piling up at my office. Oblivious, I'd walked ahead, mulling over crises that would be waiting for me when I returned.

A flurry of aspen leaves fluttered to the ground. Sarah picked up a perfectly formed leaf, ran up behind me, putting her arms around my waist, nuzzling the back of my neck. But I was still thinking about my work; so, instead of appreciating her affection, I acted annoyed as I continued up the trail.

She said, "What's your problem? I thought that you loved hiking. You even have *new* boots."

I kicked at a rock and turned away.

She stopped walking and glared at me. "I used to think that you cared."

"What's that supposed to mean?"

Taking the cigarette from her mouth, she exhaled a plume of smoke. "It means that you could think about someone other than yourself sometime. *You're* the one who said that you loved to hike. It was *your* idea to get the Kraines. *You* said that they would last forever. Then *you* got tired of them."

I charged ahead on the trail. We hiked for hours without talking to one another. Water, melting from the spring thaw, cascaded down the mountainside and spilled down the trail, creating a slippery mess. We squished and sloshed through the rocky muck. A pain pierced my right foot with each step, but I didn't want to complain about the boots.

Prior to the trip, I'd bought new hiking boots, even though the only time I'd hiked in my Kraines was on our first trip to the Rockies fourteen years earlier. But I couldn't admit to Sarah that the real reason I'd bought the new boots was because of Jenny, a young assistant district attorney.

I had made so many mistakes with Sarah. *Not one spontaneous bone in your body.* Jenny's attention had surprised and confused me.

Jenny and I had coffee a couple of times at the precinct station to go over a case. While we were meeting, I told her that I was returning to Rocky Mountain National Park to hike again and that I might even hike Longs Peak. She knew all about the Longs Peak trail. She said that most people could never complete the fourteen mile hike, turning back when they realize they don't have what it takes. I told her about my Kraines, but she said that I needed new boots

and should *stop wasting time crying over missed opportunities.*
She suggested that we meet for our next case review at
Peachtree Center Mall, so she could help me shop for boots.
We selected a pair And went to a coffee shop to review her
latest case. As we were getting up from our table, she leaned
forward and asked if I wanted to stop by her apartment for
a drink.

That's when it hit me. I couldn't rationalize my behavior
or blame it on Jenny. I wasn't naive. I liked Jenny's attention
and being with her was exciting, but the thought of losing
Sarah scared me. I told Jenny I had to get home and left.

My guilt stalked me as I struggled up the Odessa Lake
trail, and I suffered the consequences of not breaking-in my
new boots. But despite my blistered feet, I was surprised that
Sarah was still unable to keep up with my pace, so I asked
her if she wanted to turn back.

She said, "Not me. I want to see the lake." Coughing and taking several short gasps of air, she leaned against a tree. "I can do it. Can you?"

I clinched my teeth. I couldn't believe that she could be so cruel. Thinking she was mocking me, I turned away and stomped off, glaring at her as I pushed past her.

We hiked for two hours in silence before we reached Odessa Lake. Snow-capped mountains framed the sparkling frozen lake, but it was all wasted.

It was when we arrived at Odessa Lake that Sarah snapped the picture of me sitting on the lakeshore with my boots off and my jaw clenched rubbing my feet. And it was immediately after we returned home from that trip that Sarah was diagnosed with Chronic Obstructive Pulmonary Disease—COPD. She hadn't been mocking me.

Sarah's doctors told us that we were lucky. COPD is a serious disease, but we'd caught it early. If she stopped smoking, she could live a relatively normal life.

After her diagnosis, I couldn't forget how I'd selfishly thought she'd mocked me when she *really* couldn't breathe, so I completely avoided the subject of hiking, as I did with anything that I felt detrimental to her, not wanting my children to share my fate. My father died when I was thirteen.

I snapped back to reality when I heard Sarah sweeping up the bits of the crushed leaf into a dustpan. I looked at her and then at the muted television. So many lives had been lost—mothers and fathers, some who died while trying to save others—leaving their children confused by the unfairness of their loss.

It had been years since I'd thought of my father but sadly it wasn't a lapse of memory. I chose to forget.

I took my wallet off the fireplace mantle and folded back a leather flap that concealed a yellowed Elvis Concert ticket stub. I'd saved it for twenty-five years, transferring it to a new sheltered location each time I got a new wallet. Unlike the leaf, the ticket stub was one of our good memories— something I'd wanted to remember. I clasped Sarah's hand and said, "I don't want to fight anymore."

"Then stop being a jerk." She said.

"I'm sorry but..." She interrupted me.

"And stop being so defensive. It doesn't help."

"I ... I had that dream again last night and when I woke up this morning and saw the news ... Nothing makes sense anymore."

Sarah frowned. "What dream?"

"Longs Peak ... You know. I've mentioned it before."

"Not really. You've mentioned that you dream about hiking to Longs Peak, but you've never told me that it upsets you. Why?"

I pulled my hand away. "Let's just forget about it."

"You're doing it again. Quit pulling away from me. Why can't you just talk to me?"

I clenched my jaw.

"Just tell me."

I took a deep breath. "The dream always starts with me standing at the Longs Peak trailhead. We follow the trail to a stream where you suggest that we camp for the night. In the morning as we start hiking, everything seems perfect. Sunlight glimmers through the aspen leaves, smothering the trail in gold. Then your pace slows. I ask you if you're okay, but you act as if you don't hear me. You seem like you can barely walk. I look ahead and see a trail marker for Odessa Lake. I'm confused because I know that Odessa Lake is nowhere near the Longs Peak trail, but I tell you that it's okay, that we can hike to Odessa Lake and forget about Longs Peak. You seem to hear me this time and stop but then turn and trudge forward. I tell you that we can't go on, but then you scamper up a large boulder and say, *catch me if you can.* You're standing at the edge of a drop-off, smiling. You say, "Don't worry. We have our Kraines." I look down. I'm wearing Kraines. I freeze, knowing I'd gotten rid of my Kraines years before. Then your smile disappears. You look down and see that you're standing barefooted on an icy ledge. Holding out your hand, you say, "save me." I lunge forward and grasp for your hand. That's it. It's always the same. I always wake up right when you reach for me."

"You've never told me *I* was in the dream."

"I know."

"I'm sorry, but I don't understand. You've never asked me to hike anyplace since Odessa Lake, leaving me to take the initiative. Why do you think I wanted to come here for our twenty-fifth anniversary? I wanted to hike like we did before. Now you're telling me that you've been having a dream for over *ten* years, that involves me, but you haven't told me about. What's wrong with you?"

"I don't know."

"Just talk to me"

I looked away.

"I've failed you."

"What are you talking about?"

"Lots of things … I might have killed you on the hike to Odessa Lake."

"You didn't know about the COPD when we took that hike and besides, coming to the Rockies and the hike to Odessa Lake was my idea, not yours."

"But why did you save the leaf? There was nothing good about that trip."

"Don't you get it? That hike saved my life. After we came home from the hospital, I was putting our hiking stuff away and I found the leaf in my fanny pack pressed beneath the cellophane of a cigarette package. Seeing that perfectly formed leaf smashed inside the cigarette package seemed oddly symbolic. I removed the leaf, tossed the cigarette package into the trash, and tucked the leaf safely between the pages of our hiking book."

"But ..."

Sarah interrupted me, her voice escalating from frustration to anger. "If you're so worried about me, why are you dreaming about hiking to Longs Peak? You know that I'll never be able to hike that trail."

"Let's just forget about it."

"Stop doing that. Don't you care?"

Silence filled the room. I turned to the window. People were still walking along the trail, faceless silhouettes, apparently unaware of what had happened in New York, Pennsylvania, and DC. I sat next to her on the sofa and once again tried holding her hand. "I do care. When you told me you wanted to come back to the Rockies for our anniversary. I saw it as my chance to finally get things right. I know you can't really hike much, but I thought we could take some short walks and ..."

She pushed my hand aside. "I *don't* want to just take short walks. I want to hike. The doctors said I could still hike, just not hikes as strenuous as Longs Peak. Why do you keep treating me like I'm damaged merchandise?"

"I'm not. I'm just upset about what's happened. I wanted to make this trip perfect for you. And now with what's happening..."

Sarah sprang up from the sofa. Her face was flushed. "Damn you," she said. "You can't make everything perfect. You're suffocating me. I'm not a doll. I'm a person. I can't do this anymore." She lunged at the overstuffed chair and shoved it forward across the hardwood floor, banging it against the wall of windows, kicking it again before sitting on its arm with her back turned, burying her face in her hands. I heard a muffled sob.

...

I can't do this anymore. She'd said it. Why had I waited so long? "Sarah, please talk to me."

She kept her back turned and said, "You talk about love as if it were something you can organize. It's not ... not even in your *perfect* world. What aren't you telling me?"

I couldn't hide it from her anymore. I had to tell her. "I never wanted to hurt you. But before we took the trip to Odessa Lake, when I got the new boots ... well, remember Jenny, that young redhead ..."

"Frank, you didn't ..."

"No, I didn't do anything. I could have. She wanted me to. And I thought maybe I did, too. But I didn't do anything, I couldn't. When we got on the trail that day, my new boots started to rub against my feet. I was in pain after the first mile. I figured that I got just what I deserved but instead of showing you how much I cared, I ended up getting defensive, and then you had that coughing spell. I didn't know you were sick, I swear. When you started

41

gasping for air, I thought you were mocking me because I'd bought those damn boots. Then when we got home, and went to the doctor's office, and found out that you had COPD, I couldn't forgive myself."

"But if you didn't do anything, why are you feeling so guilty and why didn't you talk to me about it before?"

"At first, I told myself I hadn't done anything wrong and telling you would only hurt you unnecessarily. It was my guilt, so I needed to deal with it. After you went to the doctor, you had the COPD to worry about. Telling you that I almost cheated but didn't but felt guilty because I considered it; all seemed so lame."

"But why now? Why are you dredging all this up now?"

"I was still thinking about my dream, feeling like I'd failed you, when I turned on the television. I've wasted so much time."

"You're not perfect. You're not responsible for bad things that happen to the people you love."

"But what if I am?"

"What?"

"Responsible."

"What are you talking about?"

"…my Dad."

"What's he got to do with us?"

"It was my fault."

"What?"

"My Dad died because of me."

"You've always told me that his death was an accident."

"That's what everyone said, but I know it was my fault."

"Weren't you just a kid?"

"I was in the eighth grade. Dad had retired from the army and was working as a guard at St. Rose Hospital, where mom worked as a nurse, while he waited for an opening in one of the police departments. A winter storm moved through one night. It was one of those freaky Midwest storms—freezing

43

rain, then snow. Thousands of homes were left without power or phone service. Dad worried about leaving our home unoccupied because he knew that thieves sometimes target areas where homes had been evacuated. He told me and mom that he'd take us to Grandma's while he stayed home and waited for the power to be restored."

"Obviously the storm wasn't your fault."

"Yes, but let me finish. He let me spend the day with him and told Mom he would bring me back to Grandma's before dark. Dad had an old kerosene heater that he'd salvaged from the hospital and brought it into the house so we'd be warm. After he died, the police told us that the heater released toxic fumes into the house, asphyxiating him while he slept."

"Your father brought the heater into the house, not you. Were you with him when he died?"

"No, but let me explain. After he brought it into the house, he took me to Grandma's like he'd promised. The next morning, the streets had been cleared and school had been cancelled so I figured that Dad might come back to get me, but he didn't. I couldn't call him because the phone was still out so I laced up my boots and parka and walked two miles down the plowed but slushy roads to our house. When I arrived, I found him slumped back on the couch. I thought he was taking a nap, but he wasn't breathing. I tried the phone, but it still didn't work. I ran to the neighbor's house, screaming to get help. Mr. Jackson, our neighbor, carried Dad to his car and sped off to the emergency room."

"Your dad was probably dead when you got to him. You were at your grandma's house. It wasn't your fault."

"That's what everyone said, but the previous evening, before Dad took me back to Grandma's, I'd messed with some of the knobs on the heater, watching the flame surge bright, dim, and then bright again. I probably broke something. It was my fault. I shouldn't have been playing with the heater."

"Turning the knobs probably didn't have anything to do with it. The heater was probably defective. Your father shouldn't have brought it into the house. Did anyone tell you it was your fault?"

"No, but two days later at the funeral home, I was standing at the head of Dad's casket, in front of an easel that held a picture of him in his Army uniform. Mom had draped his old dog tags over the corner of the picture. His name was engraved on a brass plate on the bottom of the frame—Sgt. Francis Ryan Beck, Sr. Mom would look at the picture, then at me, and start crying. I knew she blamed me but didn't say anything because I was a kid."

"Frank, she was crying because her husband died."

"Maybe, but later that morning at the cemetery, a soldier gave my mom the flag that had been draped across Dad's casket. Mom told the soldier to give it to me. Dad survived two tours of Vietnam but died because of me. I told Mom that I didn't want it and she cried again."

"Your mother was crying because her husband died, not because of you."

"When I saw the towers fall, I thought of my dad. If he'd been in New York, he would have rushed into those towers just like the police and fire fighters did today. He would have tried to save everyone."

Sarah held out her hand and motioned for me to come to her. As she stood with her back to the windows, the sun silhouetted her body as it streamed through the wall of glass. I went to her. She kissed me, softly at first, then again and again, pulling me closer as she reached for the blinds-pull. The blinds crashed to the sill, sheltering us from the outside world.

Afterwards, the phosphorescent glare from the muted television diffused with reflections from the fireplace flames, creating shadows that flickered across the beamed ceiling. Stillness replaced the suffocating silence. I thought of my dream. Sarah had pulled *me* back from the *ledge*.

A harsh ring broke our serenity. It was Katie. Her flight had been diverted to Nashville.

Sarah trembled as I told her about Katie. She said, "There's so much I wanted her to see."

I looked across the valley. "Yes, she would have loved the aspen."

Sarah clasped my hand. "Let's get some air."

We walked to the trail where I'd seen people hiking earlier and stopped in a grove of aspen trees. A sharp breeze blew across the valley, sending a flurry of leaves fluttering to the ground. Torrents of gold swirled at our feet.

Clasping hands, we started up the trail, meeting other couples along the way with looks of dread and needfulness cast on their faces, exchanging glances with us as they passed that echoed a shared sense of knowing, a reordering of priorities.

A wall of clouds moved from the face of Longs Peak.

parallax (pār'ə-lāks') n. An apparent change in the direction of an object caused by a change in observational position that provides a new line of sight. From the Greek parallaxix: to change.

3

A Refraction of Time ...

settled upon the crowd as the story came to an end, enveloping the room in a hush. Everyone watched Captain Francis Ryan Beck, Jr. close his manuscript and lay his glasses on the podium. The incongruity of the image of Captain Beck, who had been introduced at the beginning of the workshop as a twice-decorated police captain, revealing so much of himself by sharing his story was not lost on the audience. Scanning the crowded conference room, the dissonance hadn't escaped

Captain Beck either. He had always thought of himself as strong, and admitting weakness to two-hundred strangers was totally out of character for him.

Frank had agreed to be the after-dinner speaker on the first evening of *The Write Way Workshop,* a weekend, self-improvement retreat sponsored by Emory University which was held at the Holiday Inn and Convention Center in Decatur, Georgia. The retreat, which focused on enhancing personal effectiveness, was part of Emory's community service programming. *The Write Way Workshop* was created by Dr. Katherine Stein to help people understand the therapeutic power of stories and to demonstrate the positive impact that therapeutic writing has on personal effectiveness. Participants included couples and individuals wanting to enhance their effectiveness both at home and in the workplace.

Frank had reluctantly agreed to be the keynote speaker when asked but was concerned that *sharing his emotions* would do nothing but cause him embarrassment; however, he now breathed a sigh of relief, sensing that the audience had, in fact, connected with his story. He didn't feel embarrassed, but instead, felt a sense of pride. The room buzzed as the crowd whispered bits of their own stories to one another. He looked at Sarah who was sitting on a folding chair close to the podium. They nodded at each other in silent approval. Many years had passed. Perhaps, they had finally gotten it right?

Frank glanced at Father Ryan, who was sitting between Sarah and Dr. Katherine Stein, the psychologist and family counselor that Leister Pharmaceutical Company funded to facilitate the event. It was Father Ryan, a parish priest at St. Michael's, who had introduced Frank to Dr. Stein after he'd met her when doing some guest lecturing in the Religion and Film course at Emory.

Father Ryan gave Captain Beck a thumbs-up and walked up to the podium. "'Tis a brave thing that Francis here has done, mind you. Facing down hooligans and the like is one thing, but standing before hundreds of people, sharing personal struggles, and offering inspiration, that's another thing altogether. Pity be the poor soul who tangles with this brave copper." Father Ryan grinned and whispered into Frank's ear. Frank laughed and hugged Father Ryan.

A stern-looking man said, loud enough for everyone to hear, "I wonder what their big secret is."

Frank, trying to defuse the man's cynicism said, "Father Ryan asked me to share what I told Katherine when she invited me to speak at this conference, but I think I've talked enough."

"No, tell us," the crowd shouted.

"She asked me how long it took me to get things right. I told her it had only taken a few moments but, unfortunately, it took me twenty-five years to arrive at the point where I understood the importance of those few moments."

Frank winked at Father Ryan. "As long as we're into confessing, don't you have something you'd like to share?"

Frank laughed. "Don't be looking so beguiled, *Father.*"

Father Ryan, looking bewildered, took the microphone. "Well, okay. It started as a joke when I first came to St. Michael's. Those of you from our parish are in on it, but I'll fess up for everyone else. I'm not Irish, but everybody thinks I am because everyone calls me Father Ryan. Ah, but me Irish brogue 'tis but a fiction you see, coming upon me when I'm feeling merry, when I see the good that comes from doing God's work. But, you see, Ryan's not my last name—it's my middle name. And tonight, the credit for my cheer goes to Captain Beck and his lovely wife—my mom and dad. You see my given name is Francis Ryan Beck, III. Yep, I'm the rogue son Captain Beck referred to in his story. When I was a teenager, I insisted on being called Ryan, seeing the whole *the third* business like an albatross around my neck. After that it kind of stuck." He gave his father a hug.

Sarah smiled with approval.

Frank told the audience that, unfortunately, the epiphanies that he and Sarah had experienced on their twenty-fifth anniversary gradually faded as they slipped back into their normal patterns when they returned home, leaving them vulnerable once again. He said, "Four years later, things took a turn for the worse, requiring that I visit with the department's psychologist. It was then that Father Ryan introduced me to Dr. Stein, who subsequently suggested that I write about my feelings *to make sense of everything*—an idea that I thought was pretty foolish, considering the gravity of my circumstance, so I dug in and resisted, only giving in to her recommendation when things seemed hopeless."

Frank acknowledged that he had in fact fictionalized some of the story's events as the story's meaning began to take shape in the years following 9/11. He told everyone that the process of searching for meaning produced his positive therapeutic benefits.

Someone questioned him as to whether it was the actual experience of that day or writing about the experience that provided the positive outcomes. He explained that the two processes were intertwined but that writing about the experience was definitely the catalyst. He said writing about the experience revealed the subtext in which all meaning is hidden. "When we're in the moment, our emotions conceal the true meaning of our actions."

A cocky-looking man stood up and asked for the microphone as if he were looking to pick a fight. "I'm happy things worked out for you and your *prodigal son*, and I'm quite sure that the next heart-warming announcement we'll get will be that Katherine Stein is your daughter, Katie. So gee, you're *all together* tonight just like Frank wanted in his story. The Beck family lives happily ever after. Ho-hum ... I didn't pay good money to come to a Beck family reunion. So help me out here. I don't get it. Tell us Dr. Stein. …Or is it Katie?

What is *The Parallax?*"

At that point, Katherine Stein stood up, looking a bit perturbed. This was not how she'd hoped things would proceed. She'd expected some skepticism about her ideas but not outright mutiny. Stories had been used throughout history to persuade and influence *other* people but little attention had been given to the positive outcomes that writing a story can bring to *one's self,* and even less to the idea that *connecting with* stories can be instrumental in improving our effectiveness both at home and in the workplace. She knew her challenge was immense and she'd have to approach the challenge as if she were peeling back an onion—the tough protective layers would have to come off before she could get to the essence that she was striving for. "That, in fact, is our plan, sir. That's what we intend to do next."

Father Ryan looked at his mother's reaction before hurriedly interrupting. "I apologize for getting us side-tracked with my antics and my acknowledgement of my dad, but I'm just so pleased to be part of this project. That's why I offered to help when Dad told me about the project he was working on with Dr. Stein, who by the way is not my sister."

Katherine Stein took the microphone back. "That's correct. It would be an honor to be Frank's daughter, but he's not my dad."

The angry man shrank back into his seat.

Dr. Stein began circulating copies of Frank's story. "We're distributing copies of Frank's story because we'd like for you to work with everyone at your tables to connect *with* this story. Please note that I said connect *with*, not think about. I don't want you to analyze it. The real question isn't: *what's this story about?* The real question is more difficult to put into words. It's a question that gets to the core of our humanity and can only be answered by the affective area of the brain, where creativity resides. Don't look at the story from a distance but, instead, move closer, connecting those feelings of chaos, confusion, and fear that characterize our lives as we search for restitution and forgiveness, yearning to *get things right.*

Father Ryan explained that Frank had spent many hours crafting his story, trying to include *what really happened* while adding elements to strengthen the meaning.

Father Ryan asked for everyone to skim through the text and find passages that might serve as metaphors in their life and explained that after their brief review they would begin to discuss their observations.

After giving everyone time to re-read Frank's story, Dr. Stein asked for questions.

A woman asked, "How important was the fact that Frank and Sarah were married on 9/11?"

Before Dr. Stein could reply, a middle-aged man got up on the far side of the room and interrupted, "I have a problem thinking that Frank and Sarah's personal problems should even be considered on a day that had such horrific consequences for New Yorkers who were directly impacted by the attack."

That comment precipitated a clamor in the crowd as they debated her point.

Dr. Stein asked the crowd to consider that having such a personal story set on a day of such international magnitude adds to the story's power because it demonstrates how layered our experiences are and how connected we are to each other.

An older man stood up and asked to speak. "My name's Clarence. I've been around the block a time or two, don't you know, and have learned to tell it as it is. I lived in New York City when 9/11 happened and, to be honest, I'm not sure it affected me any more than if I were living in Omaha. I watched the events on TV, like so many others did. I don't deserve any special acknowledgement because I'm a New Yorker. In fact, my cousin, who does live in Omaha, seemed to have been impacted significantly, perhaps more than me."

Kyle, the middle-aged man who had started the whole 9/11 debate, pulled out his smart-phone. He'd programmed it to ring at a pre-set time, so he'd have an excuse to leave the room. He said, "I'm a CEO and I live in Manhattan. I'm sorry but unless you where there, it would be impossible for anyone to understand. I think as a New Yorker, I have a unique perspective. It would be arrogant for anyone to even think they could have my insight." The room grew silent.

Finally, a young woman broke the tension and changed the subject, asking about Katie. "Why wasn't she here? After all, Ryan, *the rogue son,* was here. "What happened to Katie?"

Sarah bit her lip and started to speak, but Frank, who had taken a seat next to Sarah, grabbed her hand and said, "She can't be here."

Awkwardly, Dr. Stein quickly stepped forward and said, "Let's talk more about 9/11. That day was a watershed moment for *all* of us. I'm sorry, but I agree with the point that Clarence made and disagree with Kyle. You could have been anywhere and have been affected by 9/11."

Kyle sat stone-faced as the crowd's conversation erupted in a surge. Everyone had a 9/11 story to tell. Throughout the room people talked about what they were doing that day and how the tragedy had impacted them. They said that before Frank read his story, they'd never stopped to think about the fact that people's anniversaries and birthdays would forever share that tragic day. People's personal 9/11 stories soon monopolized the discussion.

Father Ryan asked for everyone to refocus on the purpose of Frank's story and the reason they were all in attendance—self-improvement.

One participant joked in agreement that the group needed to get back to the subject at hand so it wouldn't take them twenty-five years to figure out what it takes to *get things right.*

Father Ryan asked everyone to identify the metaphors in Frank's story—elements that could offer shared meaning.

Several hands shot up into the air. One said the story was about trust, another said it was about relationships, still another said it was about communication. Hand after hand was raised to offer more ideas. They talked about the boots, the gold scarf, the cabin, the muted TV, the aspen leaves, the mountain trails, the hikers, and Longs Peak.

A woman in her twenties, who appeared to be with the cocky young man who had spoken earlier, suggested that the group was looking at the story with too narrow of focus. She argued that she didn't think the story was only about personal relationships. She asserted that the story's symbolism could be read much more broadly.

She had barely finished her point before several voices shouted in agreement. Everyone agreed that the story helps understand our paradigms on several levels, increasing our personal effectiveness.

Marianne, the young woman who had inspired the spirited discussion, regained control of the conversation and said, "On a personal point-of-view, the story speaks very directly about marriage and relationships, but if you change the viewpoint, the story becomes meaningful at the business/professional level as well." She joked that we're still people even when we are in the workplace. "We've become a hedonistic, disposable culture," she said. "We've got to stop and take a long look at what's important."

Samuel, the stern-looking man who had goaded Father Ryan earlier into revealing that Frank was his Father said, "I'm a former CEO for a Fortune 500 company, and I can tell you that Marianne is spot-on. Businesses would behoove themselves to understand that leadership is a relationship, not a position."

Dr. Stein said, "Go on."

Samuel said, "Leadership is a relationship built on trust. I know it's a cliché but business is very much like a marriage. It's really all common sense, but it's seldom the norm."

Dr. Stein asked, "Why do you think that is?"

Samuel said, I had a professor once, who started every new class with a quote from Will Rogers—*Common sense ain't necessarily common practice.* You know, I think that idea might be the most important lesson I've learned in my entire life."

Dr. Stein smiled. "…really?"

"Yes, and I'm thinking it's the same for *The Parallax*—we need to consider the personal attributes that contribute to leadership: trust, empathy, personal values, and shared vision."

Dr. Stein, encouraged by Marianne's remark and Samuel's apparent conversion, said, "I think it's time for the next step. You've heard Frank's story, now I want you to write yours. Take a pen and one of the notepads that I've put in the center of each table and begin to write. Don't stop; just keep writing whatever comes to your mind. I don't care if what you write sounds like nonsense. Just don't stop. Keep writing. Let your subconscious take over. You may find that you might begin with something that really happened but end up fictionalizing the event as you write."

She told the crowd that she wanted them to write for forty-five minutes, and then she'd ask for volunteers to share what they'd written, telling them not worry about having to read what they've written, if they chose not to share. She said, "If no one shares, that will be okay. I want you to let everything come out onto the page without restraint. There's no right or wrong way to do this. It's very likely that what you produce will be less than perfect."

She told everyone that people often over-explain things, but that they shouldn't worry about that, telling them to *write without editing*. She said, "Embedded in what at first seems to be incoherent, scattered ideas may be feelings and memories that are important to you but have been long buried in your subconscious. Those thoughts are what we are after. They frame much of your self-concept and form boundaries for the paradigms that impact your personal effectiveness. So let's get started." She looked up at the clock. "It's 8:10. Let's say we conclude this exercise by 9 p.m. Okay?"

Bill, the young man who had heckled Dr. Stein earlier, furled his eyebrows, pursed his lips, and began tapping his finger on the table.

Marianne, the young woman who had catalyzed the discussion, grabbed a pen and notepad, and placed it in front of the young man's tapping fingers, whispering something to him as she took her own pen and began to write, leaving no doubt that she and Bill were a couple.

At 9 pm, Dr. Stein attempted to call time for the exercise, but everyone, with the exception of Bill who continued to pout, asked to be able to write for a few minutes longer.

So she allowed them to write for twenty more minutes more before asking for volunteers to share an excerpt from something that they'd written.

Hearing from no one, she said, "Our memories, both recent and distant, form the backdrop of our life. Accessing those memories is an important starting point. Often, these memories are connected to an object. These objects are particularly useful in triggering important emotions which help to access buried memories. My guess is that some of your writing tonight began with this type of object. Am I right?"

James raised his hand. "I still have a baseball that my father and I played with when I was a kid. So for me, you're correct. I wrote about baseball. I grew up playing baseball, and when I was a kid, my Dad was always there to help me learn the game. But by the time I was in high school, my dad was diagnosed with Friedreich's Ataxia, a congenital disease affecting the nervous system. After he died, the motivation and support that I'd counted on every year growing up on the diamond was no longer there, so I had to push myself to excel without him. As I was writing tonight, I realized that I was never without him. I'll read a little of what I wrote."

"Dad, if you're out there," I thought to myself, "I'm gonna need your help on this one." It was time to use what I'd been saving for all the game—all my life for that matter. As I stepped onto the mound and looked at Benny to get the signal, he read my mind—sinker, right over the plate. I came set, taking a look at the runner on third, and then I threw the pitch, just as my dad had taught me. As the pitch flew towards home, everything seemed to move in slow motion. I noticed the batter's eyes get as big as the baseball I'd hurled toward him. He thought I'd served another fastball up for him to send over the fence and send us packing. I remember thinking, "Break ... Break ... BREAK!" Then just before it got to the plate, as the batter started to swing, the bottom dropped out of it.

"Stee-riiike three!"

The crowd went wild, our bench cleared, and there was a pile-up on the mound—I was on the bottom, of course. We were state champions. As I crawled out from under the pile, I looked for my mom in the crowd. She had already begun making her way towards the field to congratulate me. I then looked to the sky and said, Thanks Dad.

"Thanks, James. I can tell from the emotion that you put into that piece that your relationship with your Dad was very important to you. I'm so sorry for your loss." The faces in the crowd looked more secure than they had just moments before. Encouraged, she asked for another volunteer. "Who else would like to share?"

Lindee said, "I'm not sure if this is the kind of object that you're talking about, but I wrote about my teenaged pregnancy. At least for a while the pregnancy was not only an object but a major obstacle. Until I began writing tonight, I never consciously realized that I had so much guilt and hatred for myself. I think now I can finally talk to my parents about my feelings and put to rest my negative thoughts and emotions. Here is some of what I wrote."

I can never thank them enough. Without my parents I don't know where I would be today. I feel like I disappointed them when I became pregnant, giving them the burden of raising my child while I finish school. They treat me as though nothing happened and tell me they are not ashamed, but I don't understand how they could forgive me. I deserve worse.

Dr. Stein said, "Lindee, it's not uncommon for someone to mistake their own guilt as unhappiness of others. I hope writing your story allowed you to understand how your parents could and *do* forgive you. Seeing things from their point of view should help with that."

Hands began to shoot into the air as the idea of sharing became less intimidating.

Andrew said, "I found myself writing about a character that feels helpless. I think that's an emotion that most of us share but seldom address. Feeling powerless seriously impacts our effectiveness in both our personal and professional lives. The story I wrote is personal, but I agree with what Sam said earlier, these emotions are relevant to our personal and our professional lives. Powerlessness is a feeling that hampers us in the workplace all the time. It can be overwhelming." Here's some of what I wrote:

"It's all going to work out. The doctor said he would start the chemo and at your age the outlook is good." Even I didn't believe what

I was telling her. It was as if I'd said what a man was required to tell his wife—a clichéd speech. But at the core, I wanted to fix this, knowing I couldn't.

"I know, babe. I just don't want to talk about it tonight, I'm kind of tired," Abby said. "Maybe we could just go to bed and talk about it tomorrow."

"Are you sure you don't want to talk now?" I replied.

"No, I'm okay. I'm gonna get some sleep," she said as she then turned away and walked into our bedroom.

I turned off the lights. The house turned quiet. A cold, bitter breeze swept from the night into the dark room as I sat praying, hearing silence.

Dr. Stein said, "That's very insightful, Andrew, Powerlessness is the same emotion regardless of the context. Once we understand that concept, we're able to improve our effectiveness everywhere."

Carissa said, "I hadn't really thought about it that way before. But after what Andrew just read, I can see that powerlessness has been a limiting emotion for me as well, and like Andrew, I wrote something from a personal context, emotions that come from seeing my grandfather suffer with Alzheimer's. It's a disease that causes pain for everyone in the family. As I began

to write tonight, I wondered how my grandmother must feel."

There he is, lying on stark white sheets. The room is dark and oppressive, pulsing beats of machines tethered to his frail body.

Here I am, sitting next to his bed, holding the hand of the man I've shared my life with for the past fifty-eight years.

The hand that I hold is the hand that put a ring on my finger; it's the hand that put food on our table, the hand that held our four children, and the hand that used to reach for mine.

The man I see is my husband, but the woman he sees is not his wife, but "a nice woman who's come to visit."

It's all that's left, but it's what I have, so when he asks each day, as if for the first time, "Can I see you again," I say "yes" and his eyes brighten once again.

Before Dr. Stein could reply, Dana said, "I also wrote

from my grandmother's perspective, but in her case, she

was the one with Alzheimer's. I was very young when it

happened, so I didn't understand what exactly was going on

until I got older and realized how terrible the disease is but

until tonight, I guess, I blocked it out. After hearing Frank's

story, I began thinking about my childhood, so I wrote

something from my grandmother's perspective, thinking about how she must have felt in the early stages of the disease."

I've always been sort of a control freak, but now I have no control. When I look to the past, I see darkness and when I look to the future, I feel a heavy weight. I can't bear to imagine the toll I must be taking on my family. Should I pretend that nothing is happening to me? Maybe I should just move out into my own place so they won't have to deal with the pain of being around me during my episodes. No, my son would never let me do that. Or maybe...

When she finished, Dana told everyone that she hadn't realized how much the memories of her grandmother were still troubling her, since it had been many years since she died.

Kyle, the middle-aged CEO who had been so rude before, stood up. A palpable tension gripped the room. He said, "I wrote something."

Although Dr. Stein attempted to conceal her apprehension, her face revealed her rising tension. She said, "Okay, what would you like to share?

Kyle's composure seemed to change from its previous arrogance to a sincere, almost childlike, innocence. He said, "I wrote about two men who represent two very different people at work. Steve Hagen is an average middle-class, hard-working family man. Andrew Kinder is a workaholic CEO who is constantly looking how to improve his company. I'm not sure what possessed me to write what I did, and I'd decided that it was meaningless until I heard other peoples' stories. I began to think about how the personal attributes of these two men might put them on a collision course, I recognized how critical changing perspective might be. As I started writing, I found myself thinking about these two very different lives. Obviously, I have some familiarity with one of the viewpoints."

5:47—the sun's rays illuminated the Manhattan skyline. Andrew Kinder loved those early mornings and the world-changing decisions that would come out of the next seventeen hours of his workday. He truly felt alive as the rest of the city slept. As he finished picking out which Armani suit he would wear that August day, he took the elevator down from his penthouse suite in the Upper East Side and walked out the front door of his building. Looking to the sky and squinting, he winced at the thought of rain as he stepped into his chauffeured Mercedes and was driven away to 27 Rockefeller Plaza, home of Kingdom Pharmaceuticals.

6:27—with the damn alarm buzzing for the third time, Steve Hagen knew he couldn't hit the snooze button again. He hated early morning, and his check at the end of the week did nothing to rouse his emotion. Only the panic of worrying about making ends meet for his wife and three kids pushed him out of bed. Stumbling across the room, he picked out the day's shirt and tie combo, dressed himself, and kissed his wife goodbye. As he walked out the door, he looked to the sky and winced, hoping that day would somehow be better than the others. He took a deep breath, stepped out the door, and made his way to the subway station.

As Kyle finished reading, he said, "I actually didn't have time to write much because I'd have to admit that I wasn't really into this program. I only registered for the program so

I could claim my trip as a business expense. I have friends in Marietta. I do this kind of thing all the time. I can always find a conference or workshop close to where I want to travel. I generally just pick up my registration materials and sit in on part of the first session, just to insure everything is kosher in case of an audit."

Dr. Stein said, "You're being awfully forthright."

Kyle said, "Frankly, I don't know why I'm telling you this. All I know is that it just hit me as I watched everyone work so conscientiously, realizing what kind of life I'd been living, acting like a pompous ass. No disrespect to Frank, but I think I was much like Frank before he wrote his story, to put it kindly, a sarcastic perfectionist. Even after Frank read his story, I doubted any of this stuff would actually work, looking more for what I found wrong with it, instead of trying to learn from it."

Dr Stein smiled. "I noticed that."

Kyle nodded. "I know, and even when Sam was talking about how we could extrapolate Frank's personal story to the workplace, I thought: *What a suck-up*. I know now exactly what he meant and agree whole-heartedly."

Dr. Stein said, "What changed your view? What started you writing?"

Kyle looked at the attractive woman sitting across the table from him and said, "As I sat disillusioned and alienated, Nicole was writing furiously. I said something sarcastic to her, which caused her to get a bit teary-eyed. When I realized what I'd done, I began to write. Now that I've seen the results here tonight, I'm going to take the time to keep writing. I can see now how writing might help me see things differently, which is often the key to success in my business." Kyle nodded at Nicole and apologized for his rude behavior.

Nicole stood up and brushed a tear from her eye. "I wasn't crying because of what Kyle said. Actually, I can identify somewhat with what he said. My grandfather just died of multiple myeloma last week, but before tonight, his death had impacted me differently. Before my grandfather died, I'd been thinking of his illness from my point of view, focusing on how much I would miss him and the toll it would take on my grandma, etc. Writing from his point-of-view helped me to understand how selfish I"d been. Here's what I wrote."

Upon hearing the news of my condition seven years ago, I had felt a small chip in my armor. The fearless self-confidence I'd possessed for my entire life had seemed useless in the face of this uncaring, senseless disease. After hearing that the disease was incurable, I'd gone numb.

I remember the doctor's words. "You still have a relatively long life left to live. However, as time and this disease progress, you'll have less and less mobility and freedom. Eventually you'll have to start using a wheelchair, as the bones in your legs will not be able to support your body. I'm sorry."

Me, the marathon runner, the cooker of Thanksgiving dinners to rival Paula Dean's, the holder of the children; unable to stand on my own, let alone walk? It was unimaginable.

Little did I know that the inability to walk would just be the beginning. The doctor hadn't mentioned the endless medical appointments that from that point on ruled my life. Gone were the easy days of retirement, not knowing what I was going to do to pass the time on any given day—every part of my life scheduled to accommodate the cancer. Mondays were visits to the oncologist to discuss my treatment plan: Tuesdays—chemotherapy; Wednesdays were lost to day-long naps, after-effects of the chemotherapy regimen; Thursdays were blood transfusions; Fridays, hours were spent at the pharmacy getting all my prescriptions filled for the coming week, and on Saturdays I would be pulled and tugged at the physical therapist's office, uselessly striving to encourage my ever-weakening body into becoming an echo of what it once had been.

What did a life come down to in the end? What have I accomplished? When I'm gone, will anyone's life be better for my having been a part of it?

Dr. Stein said, "Nicole, I'm so very sorry to hear about your grandfather. I'm sure your grief is still very raw and painful. You have my deepest sympathy. Thank you so much for your willingness to share."

Nicole said, "Yes, it's still pretty tough, but as I said writing about it has helped me see things differently—it really has helped."

Dr. Stein said, "Sometimes the real event is so painful that fictionalizing the story helps deal with the emotion, creating a distance from the real event, while allowing us to exercise control over it. Did anyone find themselves doing that tonight?"

Amanda, the young women who had asked about Katie before, raised her hand. "Frank said he fictionalized his story so I figured I'd do the same. The story I began tonight came to me as I reflected about something I'd been worrying about that turned out to be nothing. But tonight got me thinking: What if it had been something? Recently, I experienced some undiagnosed pains. I worried that I had breast cancer. Fortunately, I don't, but the fear that I experienced was real, so I chose to write about someone who experiences fear and worry. Writing this story helped me understand how worry might paralyze someone. Here's some of what I wrote."

It was a sharp shooting pain, like someone was stabbing me through the heart. Heartbreak—no, that's not what it was. It was true pain, physical pain, hanging around me like an ominous storm cloud. My chest ached—more than ached, stung—on the right side occasionally, but the left-sided pains had been escalating lately. My breasts felt tender and swollen, yet rigid and cold. Anyone could attribute these symptoms to hormonal changes a woman undergoes during and after menopause, but I suspected something more. I woke up countless times in the middle of the night with my breast throbbing, and as I would rise out of bed, the throbs always became a prickling numbness. Terrified, I'd take a shower, drenching my pain, hoping to wash away the fear.

Dr. Stein asked Amanda how she felt after writing her story.

Amanda said, "I feel like a weight's been lifted, but as crazy as it sounds, I guess now I'm still worried about Katie. Everyone seemed like they were trying to deflect the question when I asked about her before. Is she real? Or did Frank fictionalize her, too?"

Father Ryan looked at his mom and dad. They both nodded toward him in acquiescence. Father Ryan said, "Katie, my sister, died in a road-side bombing attack in Iraq in 2005. After 9/11, she joined the Army ROTC at

Emory University, where she was studying nursing. She'd always been the responsible sibling even though she was the youngest. I really was a rogue son, the stereotypical cop's son—always in trouble with no ambition. I didn't care about anything but skateboarding. I had no shame in not having a job and mooching off my parents, but Katie was different and I resented her for it. She'd always eclipsed me—a *do-gooder* who was always helping people, and I saw her as determined to accentuate my shortcomings."

Frank tried to interrupt, but Father Ryan continued. "I didn't tell you the whole story when I admitted to faking an Irish accent. You see, I grew up thinking I was Whitey Marsh, the renegade young man played by Mickey Rooney in the classic movie, *Boys Town.*"

Frank looked a bit confused and embarrassed. "Son, we never thought that about you."

Father Ryan said, "Well, maybe not, but that's how I felt everyone saw me."

Dr. Stein said, "Emotions both conscious and subconscious are the result of our self-paradigms. Writing helps bring the subconscious paradigms to the surface."

Father Ryan said, "I'm getting that now. I saw what writing did for Dad, but I never thought about how it might help me. It's funny that I didn't think about this before, but now, I think I understand the real motivation for my Irish charade. I'm trying to be Father Flanagan, the Irish priest, in the same movie, played by Spencer Tracy, who turned people's lives around. There really was a *Boys Town*, you know, and Father Flanagan was a real priest."

Dr. Stein said, "So, in a way, you've been living your story, putting a little fiction into it as necessary. There's nothing wrong with that."

Father Ryan took a long deep breath. "I suppose not, as long as we know the difference."

Dr. Stein wrinkled her brow. "...difference?

Father Ryan laughed. "… you know, between fiction and reality."

"As I see it, you're using fiction to change your point-of-view when you feel you've accomplished something good like Father Flanagan did in the movie. There's nothing wrong with that."

Ryan's expression turned serious. "It took a long time for me to forgive myself over the way I fought with Katie before she left for Iraq. I actually accused her of joining the army to make me look bad. After she died, I couldn't forgive myself."

Frank said, "Katie's death wasn't your fault, son."

"I know, but it's taken me a while to accept that truth. Tonight helped, though. I decided to write along with everyone, and guess what? I had my own *ah ha* when I put myself in Katie's place and wrote this."

Darkness had reemerged with the storm and reclaimed the sky. The moon's illusion of light had vanished, leaving me in darkness.

The clichéd belief circulated among us that "a full moon brings out the crazies." The gung-ho types would carve hash-marks in a palm tree outside the barracks to mark each moon's passing, each hash mark becoming a badge of courage, we'd beaten the crazies once again. But the mindless banter and the obsession with the moon had more to do with counting the days until our tour ended than most would admit. In Iraq, there are no front lines. You don't know who you can trust or when the light conceals a darkness that might consume you.

Katie wasn't that different from me; she had her own fears. But she had a courageous soul even as a small child. She was filled with compassion and willingness for self-sacrifice.

But I also remember that she had other dreams, just like my skateboarding. When she was an in junior-high, she talked about going to Nashville to become a country-western singer. And she could sing too. But becoming a nurse was a more direct path to helping others, so Katie put those dreams aside."

Dr. Stein took the microphone, trying to look professional but unable to hide her bittersweet elation. The program had worked. She said, "Frank, Sarah, and Ryan, I know we've talked about Katie's death before, but I need to tell you again how much I sympathize with your loss. The heartbreak from the death of a daughter or sister can never be erased."

Sarah stood and said, "It's been tough and, you're right, you never get over it. But I'd like to think that Katie is with us now."

Dr. Stein said, "I'm sure she is." She looked back at Father Ryan and said, "And Father, you should know that you're underestimating yourself. You've done a remarkable thing here, bringing everyone together, helping them connect with Frank's story. You've expressed feelings that are cut from the lathe of humanity—core emotions that are part of our shared identity. And by the way, there's nothing wrong with skateboarding. I think a skateboarding priest sounds terribly courageous."

Bill, the young man who had chided Frank and Ryan earlier, clasped Marianne's hand. His sarcastic grin had faded, morphing into an apologetic, plaintiff look. He said, "I think I get it now. Things look different from a distance, whether that distance is of *time or space*. It's only when we change our point-of-view that we gain perspective." He stood silent for a moment. "*Nashville* ... When Frank said Katie's flight was diverted to Nashville ... Did that represent ...?

Frank felt his heart race. He interrupted before Bill could finish his sentence, gratified at the young man's transformation. He cleared his throat and said loud enough for everyone to hear, "Yes, Katie's gone to Nashville."

Bill, who had initially looked pleased with himself, began to look worried, as if he felt he had intruded on something very private. Seeing this, Frank strode quickly up to the Bill and extended his hand, shaking it as if he were reuniting with someone he hadn't seen for years. And then much to everyone's surprise, Frank put his arms around Bill, hugged him, and whispered in his ear, "You don't have to make the same mistakes that I did."

Bill, stiffening, revealing some discomfort at being hugged, whispered in return, "Yes sir, I won't, sir."

Frank winked at Marianne and said, "You got a keeper here."

Sarah watched with joy, knowing that Frank, the man who had once shunned any kind of public display of emotion, had come so far.

Bill felt uneasy at Frank's show of emotion, but that feeling was quickly overwhelmed with a sense of peace, knowing that Frank had given him a new insight into himself that could help preserve his relationship with his wife Marianne.

Suddenly, the couples in the room began to hug one another, as if for the first time.

Ryan felt a profound sense of wisdom knowing that he had helped so many people. He looked at his watch. The time for the program had elapsed, but the group continued to chatter, discussing the meaning of Frank's story, thinking *with* it, examining the story's metaphors, and seeing how Frank's struggles were similar to their own. As the night grew long, the group identified the shared emotions that impacted their lives, discussing how Frank's story could help them in both their personal and professional lives. They all had stories to tell.

Ryan saw no reason to stop their enthusiasm, being content to know the good he'd done that night. So he simply smiled and said in the faintest whisper, "Ain't it glorious that all these fine couples finally understand. 'Tis a pity that most other folks be wasting their time on stuff that means nothing at all, nothing at all. Ah, they be chasing pots o' gold and such, when all the world's riches be right before them. 'Tis wondrous indeed, that all these folks before me have discovered the secret. It's put them in a tizzy, it has."

Ryan himself was in bit of a *tizzy*. But it was great seeing him enjoying life, moving toward understanding, and making connections that had once seemed impossible. Worrying that he'd never forgive himself and seeing him laced with guilt had been unbearable. It seemed that Ryan might never give himself the credit that he deserved and would never understand how much he'd been admired by his *little sis*. But, now, it seemed he might finally be able to forgive himself, move forward, and understand that he'd never been anything to me but a remarkable *big brother.*

We shall not cease from exploration
And the end of all our exploring
Will be to arrive where we started
And know the place for the first time.
                    --T.S. Elliot

4

Shards of Memory ...

pierce through your consciousness as you hear the stories, colliding with converging memories, releasing jagged emotions—shattered dreams and broken promises long forgotten. You see your past as if it were your future, sheltered with a familiarity of perspective that softens the present. You feel a resonance with all the stories, echoing promises of restitution and forgiveness.

You had thought that you knew how to control your emotions. But have you simply learned to hide them? You think of your life, your family, your job, and of everyone you love with a newfound energy.

You think about how important James' father was to him, much like Frank's father was in Frank's story. You think of your parents, suddenly realizing how everyone's parents are part of their personal story.

You think of Kyle's recognition of how differences of perspective guide our lives, both at home and at work, and of Samuel's observations about powerlessness, seeing how Andrew's, Clarissa's, Dana's, Nicole's, and Amanda's stories gave them new strength—much like Frank's story did, causing him to see things differently, which allowed him to change his self-limiting paradigms. You think of Ryan and of how he yearned to see himself differently. And finally you think of Katie.

You've seen what writing has done for others, and yearn to feel the release that they have experienced but question if writing can really help you.

You are looking for answers, but questions gather around you like sentries, keeping you safe but preventing your escape: Will writing your story help you? Could writing restore control to your life? Will you find restitution, forgiveness, and peace? Whose story is it? Who's the driving force?

Is it Frank's story, a compassionate man who is obsessed with getting things right; or is it Sarah's, the eternal optimist who tries incessantly to accentuate the positive in everyone and everything, or is it Ryan's, a man who adapts his role to the expectations of others; or could it be Katie's story, someone who has seems to have been constantly off stage attending to the needs of others while never seeing her own dream fulfilled? Or maybe it's Katherine Stein's story, a woman with a truly creative mind who often lets self-doubt be an obstacle to her success. Perhaps, it's none of these. Could it be Clarence, Bill, or Samuel? Or maybe it's Andrew, Clarissa, Dana, Nicole, and Amanda's stories together—a collective consciousness of everyone who feels powerless; or even, Kyle, the Generation Xer who had moved up the corporate ladder by detaching himself from others and had seen his employees as nothing more than pawns in a huge game until finally being able to see himself clearly.

You realize that the story is not *anyone's* individual point-of-view because the story is distilled from *everyone's* point-of-view, layered from the milieu of human experience. And then you understand that the source of restitution and forgiveness comes from seeing things differently.

You've discovered *The Parallax.*

All truths are easy to understand once they're discovered. The point is to discover them.

--Galileo Galilei

5

Author's Note

I structured this book with intentional movements in point of view to simulate what I'm asking my readers to do: experience a change in perspective and *connect with* rather than *think about* the story.

Storytelling is an integral part of the human experience. Storytellers use metaphor to make connections, revealing patterns that can help us understand ourselves and the world around us. These patterns are relevant at the personal, group, and system levels of understanding. Therefore, discovering these patterns can add clarity at home and in the workplace.

Our stories are with us wherever we go, facilitating or creating barriers to our success. Connecting with our personal story allows us to see things differently, giving us the opportunity to change our self-limiting paradigms.

I hope after reading this book you are inspired to look at your own story. It's really quite easy. People taking my writing workshops have often reacted, much like Father Ryan, saying they understood how writing might help some people but never thought much about trying it themselves. And then, after they have followed my simple guidelines and have written something, they report immense satisfaction at what they've achieved. In addition, just like Samuel in the story suggests when he quotes Will Rogers— *Common sense ain't necessarily common practice.*

Research has shown that the positive outcomes are not just psychological. It's not just about feeling better. Physical improvements can often be experienced. Moreover, it's not just about health. Understanding ourself improves our effectiveness, yielding not only personal improvements, but workplace benefits as well.

Although the workshop described in Chapter Three is fictional, the italicized passages included in that chapter are actual excerpts from participants in my writing workshops in a variety of settings. I'd like to acknowledge and thank James, Lindee, Andrew, Carissa, Dana, Kyle, Nicole, and Amanda for giving me permission to use their writing. Their willingness to share deeply private emotions is driven by their desire for others to share their experience using this process.

Begin by reading Frank's story and asking yourself:

❖ Have you experienced a major event in your life, either at home or at work that has caused *paradigm shifts?*

❖ Can you find patterns in your life that have *implicit connections* with the metaphors in Frank's story?

❖ Can you find patterns in your life that have *explicit connections* with the metaphors in Frank's story?

❖ Discuss *The Parallax* with others. Does everyone focus on the same aspects of the story? Why not?

❖ How does *your personal story* interface with Frank's story?

Finally, look for triggering prompts to stimulate your subconscious. Read books, watch movies, and share experiences with others. Regardless of your approach, it is important that you allow your emotions to surface.

The most difficult aspect of the process is committing to doing it, but the good news is that it makes no difference as to how you do it. You might choose to journal daily or write episodically. There are few rules, only some simple parameters:

* ❖ Find a time and place that allows for uninterrupted thought.
* ❖ Look for "objects" that might trigger memories.
* ❖ Let your subconscious guide the process.
* ❖ Experiment with seeing things from different points of view.
* ❖ Don't self-edit.
* ❖ Recognize that self-reflection is the primary purpose of the exercise.
* ❖ Come back to what you've written later, looking for patterns, connections, and symbolism that reveal buried emotions.
* ❖ Decide if you want to share.
* ❖ Fictionalize as necessary to create a *comfort zone.*

Most importantly, get started. Begin writing so that you can experience a change in perspective, *connecting with* rather than *thinking about* your story, *creating the change in observational position that provides a new line of sight*—the secret of *The Parallax*.

ACKNOWLEDGEMENTS

Thanking people is something that needs to be done more often, so I'd be remiss if I concluded without acknowledging those people who have helped make this book a success. For this project, I'd like to thank the following colleagues, friends, and family who have been instrumental in encouraging and supporting my writing development. I owe much to Sands Hall, Mary Gordon, Bret Anthony Johnston, Kelly Dwyer, Alan Gurganus, Marilynn Robinson, Susan Mueller, Krista Gazaway, Kelly Olson, and my students, both past and present, from whom I always learn something new. Finally, and most importantly, I want to thank my wife Sharen, to whom this book is dedicated, who has been my partner and friend in all my endeavors.

Thanks to you all.

CPSIA information can be obtained at www.ICGtesting.com
Printed in the USA
LVOW061046230113

316916LV00003B/264/P